EXTREME ENGINEERING

BURJ KHALIFA

BY ASHLEY GISH

WWW.APEXEDITIONS.COM

Copyright © 2024 by Apex Editions, Mendota Heights, MN 55120. All rights reserved. No part of this book may be reproduced or utilized in any form or by any means without written permission from the publisher.

Apex is distributed by North Star Editions:
sales@northstareditions.com | 888-417-0195

Produced for Apex by Red Line Editorial.

Photographs ©: Shutterstock Images, cover, 1, 4–5, 6–7, 8, 9, 10–11, 12–13, 15, 16–17, 18, 21, 22–23, 24, 25, 27, 29; iStockphoto, 14

Library of Congress Control Number: 2023910875

ISBN
978-1-63738-746-7 (hardcover)
978-1-63738-789-4 (paperback)
978-1-63738-873-0 (ebook pdf)
978-1-63738-832-7 (hosted ebook)

Printed in the United States of America
Mankato, MN
012024

NOTE TO PARENTS AND EDUCATORS

Apex books are designed to build literacy skills in striving readers. Exciting, high-interest content attracts and holds readers' attention. The text is carefully leveled to allow students to achieve success quickly. Additional features, such as bolded glossary words for difficult terms, help build comprehension.

CHAPTER 1
TOUCHING THE SKY 4

CHAPTER 2
TALL TOWERS 10

CHAPTER 3
DESIGN 16

CHAPTER 4
RECORD HEIGHTS 22

COMPREHENSION QUESTIONS • 28
GLOSSARY • 30
TO LEARN MORE • 31
ABOUT THE AUTHOR • 31
INDEX • 32

CHAPTER 1

TOUCHING THE SKY

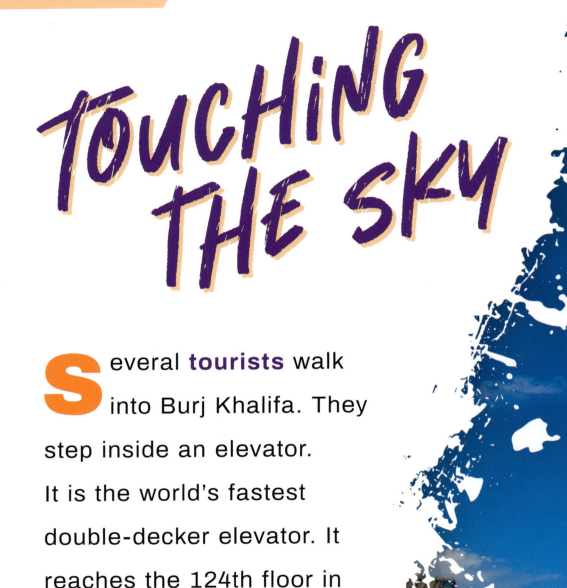

Several **tourists** walk into Burj Khalifa. They step inside an elevator. It is the world's fastest double-decker elevator. It reaches the 124th floor in one minute.

Burj Khalifa is in Dubai, the largest city in the United Arab Emirates.

The group moves to a second elevator. Video screens cover the walls. They show some of the world's tallest buildings. The elevator continues up.

FAST FACT

Burj Khalifa's elevators move at 33 feet per second (10 m/s).

AT THE TOP
BURJ KHALIFA | SKY

> There are 57 elevators in Burj Khalifa.

The Dubai Fountain sprays water to the beat of music.

The tourists reach the 148th floor. They can see all of Dubai. They take in its beautiful hotels. And they see the famous Dubai Fountain.

GREAT VIEW

Burj Khalifa has **viewfinders**. People use them to view the city from up high. They can learn about different parts of Dubai.

The viewfinders have touchscreens and videos with information.

CHAPTER 2

TALL TOWERS

People have been building tall structures for thousands of years. Often, these buildings showed off wealth and power.

In Ancient Egypt, pyramids were built as tombs for rulers. The Great Pyramid of Giza is 481 feet (147 m) high.

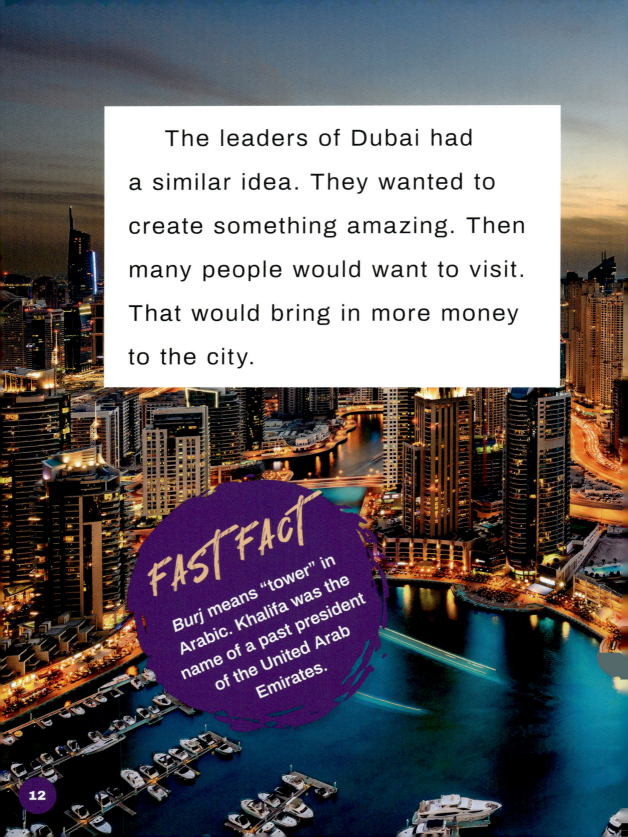

The leaders of Dubai had a similar idea. They wanted to create something amazing. Then many people would want to visit. That would bring in more money to the city.

FAST FACT

Burj means "tower" in Arabic. Khalifa was the name of a past president of the United Arab Emirates.

More than three million people live in Dubai.

Construction of Burj Khalifa began in 2004.

The leaders hired **architects**. They hired **engineers**, too. They decided to make the tallest building in the world.

WINDY CITY

Dubai is in a windy desert. So, architects wanted the tower to move with the wind. The people inside do not feel it move much. That was part of the **design**.

Burj Khalifa moves back and forth up to 6.5 feet (2 m).

CHAPTER 3

DESIGN

First, the tower needed a deep and wide base. It would support the tower's weight. For the base, workers dug 164 feet (50 m) underground.

The base of Burj Khalifa is shaped like a *Y*. That helps lower the force of wind on the tower.

Inside, Burj Khalifa is held up by a sturdy **core**. The core is made of concrete and steel. Outside, the building is made of **aluminum** and glass. It looks like tall steps.

FAST FACT
It took about 12,000 workers to build the tower. They completed it in 2010.

◀ **Burj Khalifa was constructed with 110,000 tons (99,800 metric tons) of concrete.**

The tower is not connected to any **sewers**. Waste from sinks and toilets rushes down drainpipes. Trucks collect the waste and drive it away.

RECYCLED WATER

Machines use water to cool the building. Then, the water is collected. It is used to water plants near the tower.

In the summer, the temperature in Dubai is often above 100 degrees Fahrenheit (38°C).

CHAPTER 4

RECORD HEIGHTS

As of 2023, Burj Khalifa was the tallest building in the world. It has 163 floors. People can be in 160 of the floors.

Burj Khalifa is 2,716 feet (828 m) tall.

An observation deck stands 1,821 feet (555 m) above the ground.

The tower has the highest restaurant in the world. It has the highest swimming pool, too. Each year, millions of people visit the building.

Burj Khalifa's spire alone is more than 700 feet (213 m) tall.

POINTY PEAK

A large **spire** is on top of the tower. First, workers built it inside the building. Then, they used a pump. The pump pushed the spire up to where it is today.

Burj Khalifa has 37 floors of offices. People can live in the tower, too. It has 900 residences. The tower is an amazing example of engineering.

FAST FACT
The building can hold up to 10,000 people at once.

Burj Khalifa has more than 24,000 windows.

COMPREHENSION QUESTIONS

Write your answers on a separate piece of paper.

1. Write a few sentences describing how Burj Khalifa was built.

2. If you traveled to Dubai, would you like to go to the top of Burj Khalifa? Why or why not?

3. How many workers did it take to build Burj Khalifa?
   - A. fewer than 160
   - B. about 12,000
   - C. more than 20,000

4. Why might architects want a tall building to sway in the wind?
   - A. so people inside get better views
   - B. so the building moves slightly instead of breaking
   - C. so building materials fall apart more quickly

5. What does **structures** mean in this book?

*People have been building tall **structures** for thousands of years. Often, these buildings showed off wealth and power.*

    A. outer crusts that hold things together
    B. long, thin ropes or strings
    C. buildings made from many parts

6. What does **residences** mean in this book?

*People can live in the tower, too. It has 900 **residences**.*

    A. homes where people live
    B. people who work in a building
    C. money people pay to live somewhere

Answer key on page 32.

GLOSSARY

aluminum
A light metal that looks silver-gray.

architects
People who make plans for buildings.

core
A sturdy, central part of a building or other object.

design
A plan for how to make or build something.

engineers
People who use math and science to solve problems.

sewers
Underground pipes that carry water and waste.

spire
A structure on top of a building. It is often shaped like a cone.

tourists
People who visit a place for fun.

viewfinders
Devices that make faraway objects appear closer.

TO LEARN MORE

BOOKS

Bowman, Chris. *Skyscrapers*. Minneapolis: Bellwether Media, 2019.

Murray, Julia. *Burj Khalifa*. Minneapolis: Abdo Publishing, 2019.

Newland, Sonya. *Extraordinary Skyscrapers*. North Mankato, MN: Capstone Press, 2019.

ONLINE RESOURCES

Visit www.apexeditions.com to find links and resources related to this title.

ABOUT THE AUTHOR

Ashley Gish has authored many juvenile nonfiction books. She enjoys learning and sharing information with others. Ashley lives in southern Minnesota with her family.

A
aluminum, 19

B
base, 16

C
concrete, 19
core, 19

D
Dubai, United Arab Emirates, 8, 9, 12, 15

E
elevators, 4, 6

F
floors, 4, 8, 26

G
glass, 19

S
spire, 25
steel, 19

U
United Arab Emirates, 12

V
viewfinders, 9
visiting, 12, 24

W
waste, 20
water, 20

ANSWER KEY:
1. Answers will vary; 2. Answers will vary; 3. B; 4. B; 5. C; 6. A